First Printing, 2018
Wild Cabbage Books
wildcabbagebooks.com

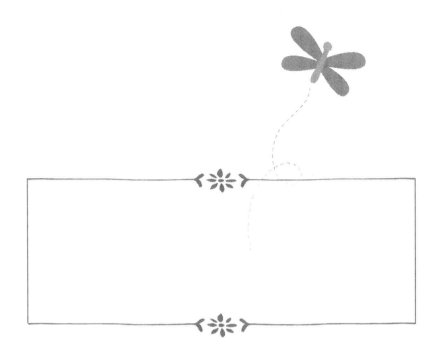

Each of us is limitless; each of us with his
or her right upon the earth.

– Walt Whitman

This above all: to thine ownself be true.

— Shakespeare

Excellence is not an act, but a habit.

– Aristotle

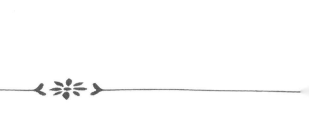

No act of kindness, no matter how small, is
ever wasted.

- Aesop

The way to be happy is to make others so.

— Robert Ingersoll

Be happy for this moment. This
moment is your life.

- Omar Kayyam

Peace is always beautiful.

- Walt Whitman

The greatest mistake you can make in life
is to be continually fearing you will make
one.

— Elbert Hubbard

Bloom where you are planted.

- 1 Corinthians KJV

Made in the USA
Middletown, DE
19 June 2019